THE SHAPE OF A TULIP BIRD

CHRISTOPHER HOPKINS

Poems by Christopher Hopkins
Clare Songbirds Publishing House Poetry Series
ISBN 978-1-947653-72-6
Clare Songbirds Publishing House
The Shape of a Tulip Bird © 2019 Christopher Hopkins

All Rights Reserved. Clare Songbirds Publishing House retains right to reprint.
Permission to reprint individual poems must be obtained from the author who owns the copyright.

Printed in the United States of America
FIRST EDITION

Cover image © 2019 Lisa Gane

Clare Songbirds Publishing House Mission Statement:
Clare Songbirds Publishing House was established to provide a print forum for the creation of limited edition, fine art from poets and writers, both established and emerging. We strive to reignite and continue a tradition of quality, accessible literary arts to the national and international community of writers, and readers. Chapbook manuscripts are carefully chosen for their ability to propel the expansion of art and ideas in literary form. We provide an accessible way to promote the art of words in order to resonate with, and impact, readers not yet familiar with the siren song of poets and writers. Clare Songbirds Publishing House espouses a singular cultural development where poetry creates community and becomes commonplace in public places.

140 Cottage Street
Auburn, New York 13021
www.claresongbirdspub.com

Contents

There's a Fist Where the Heart Should Be	7
Magpie	8
The Empty Chapel of Your Eyes	11
The Shape of a Tulip Bird	12
Hospital	15
The History of the Colour Red	18
I See, Only With the Light From Fires	21
My Heart is a Failed City	22
Inside the Tear	24
Listen to the River	25
In Paleness	26
Away	27
Stars in Pocket	28
Arrival	29
In Another Version of Myself, I am a Happy Mess	32
Mustard Seed	35
The First Light	36
Navigator	39
Prelude to Night Swimming	40
My Language Has Run Out of Broken Bones	42
Rock Pool	44
Yellow Beak	45
Weather Bell	46
Fracture	47
Metal & Salt	49
A Portrait in Starlight	50
Otter's Back	51
My Dear Night Beside You	52
Debris	55
The Nature of Love	56
Ancestors	57
A Boathouse	58
Reader & Listener	59
Let the River Run Red	61
We Washed the Blood of Childhood From Our Faces	62
Love / West / Atlantic	63
White feather	65

Acknowledgement & Thank you

I would like to thank the following publications - Ghost City Review, Barren Magazine, London Grip, The Journal (UK), Thanet Writers, Marble Magazine, Picaroon Poetry. Words for the Wild & Fly on the Wall Press.

Special thanks to Angela Dye, Lisa Gane, Amanda Oosthuizen, Katy Evans-Bush, Rachael Ikins, Shirley Bell, Maggie Harris, Rosie Johnston , Jeffrey Allen Hanson & Rosemary McLeish.

Cover image by Lisa Gane
@twentythreebydesign
www.facebook.com/twentythreebydesign

For my love, Louise.

There's a Fist Where the Heart Should Be

The grain in the shape of a bay
I remember.
Searching for a flicker in the static flesh.
Snow feathers
scattered to the sea
of our wombing storm.
The body doesn't keep its secrets.

We watched a little death
in the marble swell.
Holding hands in the black & white
that shimmer of sound,
shimmer of night,
only the human in you
can't help but look,
to find a face,
fixed to see a pattern
of eye and mouth.

It takes two to check the scan,
to look into the spring of heaven
and not see a face of deity,
    the absent echo of an unborn heart,
and tears deepen the blue roll
in lily creases.
Nobody knows what to say.
    What can they say?

Out of the well of our embrace,
my echo in a silent nod
to the sorrys said.
I have an ocean of love for you
but there is no shelter on the ocean,
there'll be no shelter from this.

You'll say, your body haunts you.
It haunts us both.
The tiniest muscle gave out
and broke us.

Magpie

An act of lunacy,
hunting for change for the car park,
feeling sick
and homesick.

Old men in the queue
talk of an ill wind in their beloved heart
and I just wish they'd hurry up and pay

—when a magpie
comes calling
                from the conifer—

and like a pistol draw
I'm searching for the second.

        There will be no girl
        there will be no boy

        tight in my palm
        silver and gold

        your name
        is my secret.

I'm so in love with my dead.
My little black love.

We share our chemistry,
the little twist of helix - fixed in blood.
My blood,
still inside you

and I drowning
in the rush I hear,
the torrent from a useless heart.

I was the body of spring and maidens milk,
I believed in the blossoming stars
in the garden-dark of a new year
and on a skip-stone flash
I made the labour of wishing
my craft.

When your head lay in my lap
you could hear the twice beating,
I walked with two souls singing.
Oh joy,
how you struck with such purpose,
the heart-stone weight
of motherhood,

and now
on this tarmac ground
I flinch with every remembrance
the certainty of their sorry.
Their paper towel grins,
dressed ready
as if for clipping wings.

At this moment
no one else dare pass,
no one else will grieve

but us.

> *If* life is a feather
> black
> or white,
> then death
> is a blinded bird
> singing to the night.

The Empty Chapel of Your Eyes

And with a dying of the softest light,
the bed-lamp calls to the north stars
as the caged bird, closed up
to the swallow-tailed will.
You are here
& you are not here.
Nested & empty,
centring a view
to a palm of solace,
your candlelight vigil,
and silent in the colour blue.

What will your searching tell you
that you don't already know?
Only an anatomy of my sciolism.
It will bring no light,
no gracer light reflection
to the empty chapel of your eyes.
My love, look at me.
Please, don't think I do not love you.
It is the stars that disappoint me,
not you.
It is the universe that moves apart,
I am right by your side,
though my dialect, ancient to yours.

You are the huntress.
I am Orion's frozen corpse.
Stiff-boned with action.
My club of vows powerless
to your course.
Tonight, all the heavenly bodies
are without spines, without warmth.
There is no freedom in the cold.
The world is haunting you now,
the night sounds
have climbed into bed with us.
I try to lift the spirits,
come to comfort, stand & shoulder the weight,
but I'm shouldering a box to be buried,
and death is not finished with us yet.

The Shape of a Tulip Bird

I am everyone
at the level of my beating heart,
though mine takes on the shape
of a tulip bird,
the knocked dove to the dying dirt.

This is not a journey
to a crossroads,
or
for one day
a dance on keepsake
reflections.
This is my abiding silence.

The song of my chapel,
that sweet seed-bell,
has silenced,
and while he sleeps
in the white of its peace,
in the dying hum of its peal,
I ask—
> *why did you*
> *stop   becoming you*
>
> *my child*
> *in love   in endings.*

Am I the shepherd's body
or the wolf?
Am I the white sun?
I know I am the vigil
of the living,
the unburied
& the dead.

I tasted that happy madness of love,
the flame-fretted ache,
that gentle perfection of worry
only
a mother can make.
I felt the electric join
of womb to soul,
ache to healing.

Praying hands
shape a hollow heart.
An empty seed
from where the rubus lines have come.
The sealing borders
of my middle youth,
tangled permanence
of living.

I'll bleed you out
like a rose
breaking.

Hospital

The only colour is outside the room.
Spring's primary colours
to the nothing of the room.

Another sorry said.
This one feels   *heartfelt,*
practiced in being
said   a hundred times before
                god knows
                        how many times today.

      You are talking
      we are listening,   you are both talking
                                    and listening.

On the nurse's desk,   there are waves of papers,
        lapping at the dark blue jacket of your medical notes,
                shifting with the conversation.
            Photocopies of   forms,
        templates,
            a thousand times distant from the original.
            Black lines of tick boxes,
        of margins
                            are lost
    to a mist like evaporation,   the fibre hairs
                            of cheap paper,
                            of a fog coming in.

      You are talking
      we are listening, you are both talking
      and listening,
      I'm holding your hand like the blind.

           I watched each face
           come into the waiting room;

           young women alone
                you don't know it yet
                but how brave you will be.

      For the couples who came in, the world
      hangs around the torsos
      of the mother;
      either colour in their cheeks and full hair

>   or colour in their eyes, behind
>   steady margin lines
>   of black eye liner,
>   a bet to themselves,
>   defiant to their grief.
>
>   Either way, good news or bad,
>   behind each of the new father's eyes
>   there's a frightened little boy.
>
>   I catch the eye of one disquieting son -
>   My thirty-eight years to this green boy,
>   more than half the age of this spring devil
>   with all the young strength in his arms,
>   to carry his child above him,
>   all that time for him
>   to master being that
>   jack of all trades,
>   to disappoint,
>   to love,   to give her away.
>
>   I have no wisdom for sitting here.
>   The colour outside is becoming a mosaic.

A plan is discussed,
agreed,
      nodded to by me.

A blister pack and time is handed to you.

>   The first step in becoming one,
>   from us.

The History of the Colour Red

Kingfishers in the staining
        take in the light & glow,
                casting pools of curled comfort
    in fox-red and blue.

They wait with me,
        watching from their simple scene
        above the door.
Watching for flashes of life,
        seeing what others cannot
                beneath the patched light,
upon the river from the door,
        way down on the hall way floor.

I am in the black of dreaming,

my body as the starling darts
        whose form I catch
                through the clear fractions of glass,
their bolt & rear,
        to the kite tail lines on the wire,

shaping my loneness,
        my thoughts of punishment.

But they carry each other, on the wing
        about the blowing thatch of this house.
                Penned together in the poor catch,
twisting in their patch of sky
        like a body pushing out the dead.

An hour after work,
        waiting for you in a familiar wilderness,
                from my seat on the first few stairs
up to our bed,
        where I catch the kingfisher's light,
                wishing to be in the warmth
of its red yolk, that mercy,
        for my heart to be expelled, to be held
                by a better being than myself.

The Alice band of light is fading
        to the west and a gauze of night is
            a fathering dark.
The blotted reds start to cease,

        the flesh of a backward vine.
            Now the kingfishers
       have gone to their cutting,

a shoal of fish come swimming,
       in with the lights of your parking car.

In with the breeze
       you step to your side of the riverbank.
           I sit here in the dusk of your eyes
on my nettle ground
       with the traces of red beneath me,
           traces of a thread between us.

Do you think of blame as I do?

I See, Only With the Light From Fires

In idle moments, *where I am found,*
I grieve in a lesser black than you,
a witness to your love.

These weeks have passed like a promise
in the after-life
of our bed-light,

dreaming of a sunflower crown—
                as if caught by rain,
wet hair of the faceless child, the blossom
rose of being,
from your bud of not knowing.
                All this dreaming in mind
with our backs turned on one another.

                The dead sleep in our grieving arms,
dull to the limbo wastes where their names are called.
It is the living love who cannot find their way,
until a time when we last say their name,
when death becomes its place of rest,
and the less we see with the light from fires.

I can make an angel sing in a finger rub
on the glass's rim,
and make you cry with crack of vile
from my foul mouth—pour the amber sea,
smelling of the earth,
down on my cinders and up come the flames
singing

for the little wings of womb,
the grim oyster between your hips,
for the horror of your love.

It is not just the dead who fill oblivion.

The dreaming took root in you
quicker than my boyhood seed,
and we'll come back to it, the vow
and promise,   I'll come back
to my ticking master
as like a beaten dog with all the love
in its eyes,
wringing the love from our bedsheets
or out the blood of a child.

My Heart is a Failed City

My heart is a failed city
      this body, the broken country.

Every day I reroute myself to be,
to be walking , to eat
the flex of breath,

the two of me,
      the mouth to the world
      and eyes to the mirror.

I hear & see in static, a hiss smother
over traffic & voices,
gone cathedrals
      in detached horizons of snowfall.

      All the heaviness is at my centre.
This den of heaven's gravity
is a physical hole of absence.

      Every millimetre   of nail
      or tinder of hair
      growing,

      is my body
      taunting me,
      the beggar of queendom.

I can tell you,
no light fills the fallen spaces.

My heart is a failed city,
this body,
the broken country.

Inside the Tear

              I called my mother
to tell her,   let her know,
hoping to talk   this through

safe   under the curve of her wing,
the bulletproof softness of mother.

She   did not   understand me.

Her wing was too stretched and hollow
and the light passed right through it.

'Maybe you can take comfort knowing
       it was early   in the sense of things.
Every new moon is now a spring,'
I should pull myself up on the
        withers   of   some   fucking   horse.

My wings are tired
and I have yet to find
my island.

Listen to the River

Turbulence
in this stretch of water
has always called for company.
Either the swerve of lights from the townland
or a restful stop of a knot.
We all come to the river,
to the glasswork of the flooding mouth,
the flicker of the crushed can moon,
seduced by the witchery of the brackish water,
pre-ocean lush of a quiet life.
A waterline of confluence, the past
to present time.

I come to hear the absence singing,
that cruel song that rhymes

I love you

—or when the wind comes twisting in Autumn,
the ripple movement from the beginning of rain,
like the water's return to the boatman's turning -

My name is heaven.

The day-swimmer is blessed with the numbing
of questions by the coldness of the water.
And the night-swimmer, an eating mirror.
I know how long the water waits
as the tide is turning, I've set my watch to it.
Though these contours have no master
past the clock,
and the shallows look deeper
by the simple tricks of the light,
this black fuse
running through the city,
that's never lit.

In Paleness

I grieve
in the company of others
as the moon.
Full and round
or to my dagger point.

A quiet smile
to stop the rattling
of sympathies,
or the sorry robes
put upon my shoulders
inadvertently
too small.

In the dry air of the office light,
beneath such careless
hands of stars,
I sit amongst the forest-night,
with no form but paleness.

I pull the excel sheets
up, over my shoulder,
and I'll bed down here
beneath
these covers.

Away

From the warmest room
we think about life outside
for the first time in months.

Maybe for a time we'll confuse
the unsayable beauty
with the nothings of God,
let the sunlight pass right through us.

Maybe for a time we'll be away from here
on a needle's swing of distracted joy,

feeling the footling sting
of a different wind, taking everything
from the tear,
back to nothing but our salt.

Stars in Pocket

Unmoored from the town,
with all the stars in pocket.
I travel with no wiser bible of my homeland,
decoding the dying tongue of night,
the red eyes of the stalking day.

      I didn't know the breeze
until out from land,
this touch of a sweeter chill,
the air from an unmothered hand.

Cotton folds in the churning wakes
spread, out from our breaking spur
sparks of rainbow
over a spectrum cold of green & grey.

      It's all a welcoming
from the boxed sea-night,
the lullaby of the engine's purr
and the whistling winds
are the lost bird's prayers.

Arrival

We came in with the herring.
The arrow line wake of our ferry,
making a swill of the salt dark.
Circle stirs of the un-yellow froth,
met by the turn of strain in round
wicker pots,
lay a hundred eyes
of iris brown.

I'm being stared down
by the foreign bulk of an uplands.
By a cloud range
born in a heartbeat of the Arctic.

I am already bathed in this place.
Infant-like.
Absorbing the inherency,
the largeness of the undisturbed.
There's a freshness smell
even to the dying, here.

Weathered poached houses
of thick yeast outer walls,
their set square windows
of lake shiver glass,
stand as stacked rows
of silver in approach,

shaping as if a giant's dagger,
fallen on the foothills
from a long forgotten slaughter
of its fairy-tales,
from some distant epic,
lost in the knocking of rope on mast.

It's the whole landscape striking at me,
the many horizons;
base colours
of the wolf eared mountain,
the green wetness of the kingdom,
the sea's pearl soot,
to its breath
of pencil line whites.
All in a calmness with each other,
all as gentle as a breath
between prayers.

It is this I cannot understand.

I consider,
—being born of water—
the schist
and hammered shell,
split to knife edge specks
and rounded numb
in the throws
of a belly sea,

how long beauty takes
to tear itself apart
and re-appear
as beauty.

Nature never builds antipathy,
horror is just in its nature.

We are grain
in an inconsistent froth.
Some waves crest
with a quarrelled call
of the journeyed tern,
others
under the skeleton
of a dog.

In the transit
of beauty,
some have fallen harder
than others.

In Another Version of Myself,
I Am a Happy Mess

Death lives on the coast.
Its thick with it.

Where there is death
there is the light.
Where there is suffering
the sparkle tide
blinds the eyes to it,
to all the subtle changes
of how life tolerates its salt.

Hard carcass shells,
toughen skins of daisies,
all beneath the white curve
of a gentle front,
the horse mane whisped out
from the belly clouds.

Beauty can't be trusted.

Listen
to the right pitch
       and you'll hear it,
exposed in the hissing withdrawals of tides.

What we devour, as the imbued tourist,
is thrilling as the path of tongues
to first kisses.
All Nature is,
is urge & returning.

It was wrong to come here.
Wrong to escape your palace
under a stealth of sun,
loosening my grip on
the wish bone,
'cause all the compass hand will do
is swing from heart —to head—to my low ache,
the pointing finger of my own
silent hand
of every drink,
every cigarette I touched
before I knew of you.

All the windfall bruises,
every bad spell which made
my body unready for you.

Sorrow
is like settling water.
Affliction finds your lowest point,
  your deepest well,
   and l am singing up from it.

   I sing for
   all those who sleep
   with one eye on their body,
   nervous of nature,
   a nervousness of touch.

In this moment,
as if its listening
here, in this language of land,
the breeze brushes the hair
from my face.

There is a heat
to the ground.

Mustard seed

In the kingdom
of welcome,
a house of
white stone
by itself
in summer.
An inverted wing
of landing.
Come down,
       come down,
so you feel
the mustard grain
pushed down
under
your feet.

The First Light

Seabirds are impatient
with the dawn.
I stir
to step bare foot
upon wooden tread,
in a darkness itself
almost living.
A slow glaucous light
is birthed,
and horizons find their way to me,
breathing the thinner blue
in the moments
before the pastel strike
turn to the mortar blue.
A frosted pane
in the dwelling's high
looks back to land
to shine a copper flame,
darkening the landing
by its brightness.

A breakfast of eggs,
bread,
coffee.
Dressing
in the honey sun of our room,
before stepping out
to the freedom flare of the nickel salt,
by the waves ungoverned by a moon,
gulls crying like their saviour born.
I am lost
in the power of now.

It starts unseen,

soft as a lyric 'round the head,
I don't see it, as the cross wind
between the drifting birds,
or more the kindling smoke
of a newborn fire.

Your name comes to me.
Your name   comes to me,

*the sudden
and the flood.*
A sun ray of a coldness. A strange heaviness.
Forgetting is a shiver,
taking my wage of breath in a soured thought.

This was the first day
where you did not stir
with my limbs,
walk in my thoughts.
The first day
you were not the first idea,
as if I mislaid you in foolishness,
if your spirit emptied.
I'll tell myself in an amnesty of a moment,
the spirit had found its wings,

curious to this stranger's place,
then back to the chest
to fill this vessel with all it has seen,
sweeten the milk.

Grief wounds you
where you have never
been wounded,
where other light doesn't reach.

I breathe you in,
fill my lungs with you
wanting to drown in you.

It's so easy to inhale,
so unlike
the vinegar of the city.

This sky
we are beneath,
with all its promise,
its side-stepped spirits,
is the most
vitreous of heavens,

as if almost
breakable.

Navigator

A hawk head of a sun.
Neck line & forearms
in a wind hushed reddening
from the grip
of an unexpected heat.

I watch you
in this flipped world.
Navigator.
Stargazer
to the flicker constellations,
the flare of a flash gun sea
(the many hands of light).

You are auburn gold
in the rub.
Unpicked by scavengers,
by questions.
Breathing
like an ordinary day.

The shadows & light
play by your side,
the day & the wind
through the honeysuckle,
a beautiful veil falling
and un-falling in the space
between you & I,
our
other traveller.

I watch you
in this flipped world.
You are woven gold,
my vision.

Prelude to Night Swimming

The night blue is a ring above us.
Stars are all small number,
an eye,
a foot
of waking deity.
Chalk blades
on the sea appear
as the warm wind picks up.
Black clouds,
in their hammock of horizon.
It is Autumn fever
& Summer waters at once
    (as if a magpie's heart alone is a stone,
    and flower in the company of others).

Flash & mute at first.
The dangle-flicker
of a silver cross
caught by the corner eye.
Then the roll of noise to be sure of it.
Stiffened light,
a branched star, cracking.
    A brightness beyond experience.
It was as bright and wild
as the madness of love for my closest
stranger.
A shock to the black,
acid crack & air cracking,
with thrones of clouds
rolling closer and closer -
form of curve and triad colour,
the black & blue & flashed,
and flashing -
rain drops so heavy
the earth moves in receiving it.
    The backside of the moon appearing
at our feet. Wet clothes,
crowning our skin,
    warm & tight
    & perfumed,
    like another's hand of intimacy.

And as quick as it came,
the frailty of the flash

returns to its black hard state.
Creation is refreshed.

>   Rewind the lightning,
>   and I'll watch again
>   the light's transition,
>
>   the ink pad & the trauma,
>   the boiling seas.
>   The moment life sparked
>   and death
>   feared.

We waded in, up to our waists,
and the sea lifted us.

My Language Has Run Out of Broken Bones

Eyes are beginning to see.

On the last breath of night,
the indigo of the west
leaving a print of a paper skull,
its wicked tongue of seabirds.

The Sun has come for us.
Scraped itself
out of the mirror.
Another life in parallel,
opened up on the bedroom wall.

I read the braille of the wicker weave.
A story of the young woman
who sat here naked to the stars,
skinned & god deep,
restless,   shaken out,
always that minute towards midnight
on a New Year's eve.

I have asked myself if I gave love too easy,
then pinched myself hard. To think how much
I love this speck, this wonderful nothing,
nothing of birth.

> Cheap books,   cheaper wine,
> were black ghost followers,
> shadows to the white tail
> of the familiar haunting.
> —*Carrier of death.*
> *Exile of love,   mother of earth.*
>   —*Broken bones of language.*

A minute towards midnight on a New Year's eve.
Now   a minute past.

          This place,

this place must be
where the world comes to grow old,
still unknowing of what
it is looking for
but finds a pleasure in the light,
against a moon-pressured sea

and a love of land, found by a crooked
map of flowers,
among the paths dusted
with their lions' teeth,
against the ticking rocks in August heat.
All this dried,   desiccated remains,
ready to spark to life
with the sign of any rain.

I hope that you heard
my voice, in passing,
still happy-tongued, and
felt the sun of hands on the warm low hill,
when dreaming
was burrowed with you.

Rock Pool

Our step,
unsteady on the atlas rock.
Arching toe to heel
on iron stone.

I am smiling with you,
smiling
& forgetting,

coming and going
with the buck
of the leather kelp straps
'gainst the fleshy plump clots
in their sun fixed gloss,
all bright in
penny-blood colours,

or the tissue ribbons
of young green thallus
that woo limpet orange stars,
rough as cats tongue.

Wavelets of past hood,
a shade of childhood
looking in.
A flash of sun,

the pan-colours of my mirrored face,
eyes of x &
the smile of y.
There, my
mother smiling.

You catch me from falling.
My eyes closed in the moment,
      held.
It passes with our eyes closed.

      The inter-land surrenders.
      Waves of angel wings
now drowning silver,
the returning heaven, a breath of escape
for the small life confined,

and I am caught thinking
of the incoming rush
of that kiss
absent between us,
and it pulls the heart under.

Yellow Beak

'Cross the sands
we pass a carcass of a sea bird,
dried
and belly burst.

An unnatural
and recognisable form.
The worked yellow flint
of its beak,
the sand-washed grain
of a wish bone
whiter than the torus nest of feathers
that once was its chest.

And there gather
the choir
that sung its death;
shaped pellet trails
    and bottle tops,
the weathered beads
of a nameless colour,

the fish & shrimp
of its plastic suppers.

How the down shivers
in the intimate winds.
A body still un-rid
of a dying breath,
a ghostly twitch
of a starving brimful,

a stomach full of death.

The Weather Bell

A fisherman inspects his nets to a stay line whistling.
A breeze singing no-ones name.
A gentleness of thread across finger & palm,
as if he is counting his prayers, thanks
of what he knows of his kingdom,
to his someone listening.

Sure of his skill & practice, unsure of his luck
& the weather bell.
Leting himself go unto the promise, with the white wail
of mischief at the stern of his church,
all asking for favour,
only the line will beg for it, with each new haul,
asking if attention has been paid,
or if the calls from other mouths were louder.

Fracture

A hundred years
to smooth this pebble down,

for it to split
under my foot,

the finder of fracture,
lines against strata.

The pulse in the crack,
the small spear head turned

on my shame
in breaking the beautiful.

Gone the dynasties of full moons
& the seas

its carer.
My lumber,

over the brushing hand
as they were loved.

Metal & Salt

A chipped nail as the rust,
your crows' feet and
an indent of a chicken pox mark
shadow in the sun-late blush.
You beautiful moon.

The sun

hangs
as the wrecker's light.
(
Yielding and flux,
bleeding in our colours,
)
blinding
in oxide wash,
      the specked
              gold.
An old link chain,
tacky hands from pebble hunting.
The painted skull
of mooring post.

The air is eating
at us all,
      and the
      birds
      all point the same way.

A Portrait in Starlight

For all the days where I couldn't tell
the bellies of night gulls from the stars,
where my chest ached so much with the clot of loss
and the phantom smell of milk under my nose
from a muslin shroud soaked through with it,
with false motherhood,

I could not for the hell of it, see beauty,
        only the white of its marble.

Though *love* became a darker word,
a sometime windfall of marrow
from empty arms or the skeleton of a bull,
for all the amens that trespassed on our lives
from an unknowing heaven,
us, like fishing boats stained, reeking of their labour
by the fight given from the sea,

    we   were not   to blame.

I am finding my strength
but not yet my peace.
We should have shared in our fears.
I could have told you my tear thoughts
of this lifetime and help
un-break you
as the father, use the loving milk.

In the poverty of starlight,
the flicker and song, somehow
they show all the gifts that are given.
See the good of the world.
Even in our blackness best,
in this starlight,
I see your river glass glint from depths.

Spark your brightness back
and think of life as that
which makes up the light.
Shine in returning. Thrive in shining,
let our light be from the living,
and make the star-bright
more than the wishes
of other people's lives.

Otter's Back

       We walked the otter's back
over to the narrow town,
       the tide receded to sail the world.

       The sands catch their breath,
hard as cobble stone under foot,
       working our ankle & sole.

       Curlews sow for lugworm in the ozone
as we talk of the simple things.
       Floured whitebait, wine,

       the wishing light,
lost in the comfort
       of company.

       Our shadows, now on the causey.
Their form bobbing ahead,
       stretching years ahead of us

       on the granite way,
with a solace of headstones,
       side by side.

My Dear Night Beside You

Homed to the tap-household.
A harbour of acid glass,
halo clouds of weightless silver
above the seaweed,
the colour of shadows beneath our feet.

A backstay of the sun's late fuse
comes to the room as the wanderings
of the burning bush,
the steel pearl's
olive touch.

I've watched the knot behind your ears
fall in ribbon arms over the afternoon.
Pulled on
and loosened by the drink
& salt bread.

A rhythm of joy
under the breath,
a staggering happiness
as if still hiding
from itself.

You are where the sea bone
is breaking.
Talking of nature and the light
as Mary's robe is falling,
where white marigolds
come rushing in,
touching our feet in a rare feeling
of liberty,

a false consciousness
of eternity,
when it is a day
simply repeating itself
in the syntax of weathering,
on rock limbs,
shell skin,
a labouring sea.

The light changes
but the drink doesn't.
High tides

of whiskey and water
and a beckoning tongue
of the carving moon
and your rhythm
is the rattle of armour.

Your thoughts
are of the blackbird's song
and it soon becomes the only language
travelling from hand to mouth,
stumbling
when happiness makes herself
unavailable.

The seafarers go
where horizons dip,
colourless, until they share
their warming nebula,
their petal stars of home
and *my dear night beside you*,
now you are lost
among the island lights,
you are nothing but pity's drunk.

Debris

Cataract of the sea-rubbed plastic
weaving as Israel's body in the waters.

The drowning spot against
the harbour wall

where eddies and elegies fold
in honey-glass curves.

Somehow the bottle remains buoyant,
defiant to the natural.

A stubbornness even in
its exile, this alien,

this little boat
of oblivion.

The Nature of Love

I am wool-gathering about this place,
this land
under a tempest's blows.
Quarry of cloud faces,
rough pour of silt veins.
The Mother, 'destroyer'.
The absolute of bend & break.

The shingle steep is singing.
The unreachable strata
at the boiling edge of the crown
as words are pregnant in the mouth.
Armoured land, perished
to a flint swell of the last tide
falling
in a drowning light
of the gutter spill.

A pebble tossed here
could be as lethal
as David's sling.
How something so small
could hold
such damage.

There was no knowing,

where we were caught,
there was no knowing
the ground was at our feet,
just beyond our reach,
our thought
of rock-bottom.

Maybe the nature of love
is to be tossed,
as simple as that,
and to hold dear
what is left
after the rasping pull has been,
in the drying of wings,
a resettling of spirits,
what is taken in dreaming
and left in waking.

Ancestors

The runestone's colour has gone,
though the wildflowers
are still in its mouth.
The dead still boast of themselves
from the worked plane.

A translation,
typed on the small
white card, tilted at its foot,
its corners—
sharper than a cutting tool.

A thousand dead years have passed
for that stone
without its masters,
while the pinned winged bugs
lament their century's end.

What will be left of us,
when all our footprints of zeros and ones,
as brief as their ether charge,
have gone, what from us
will they pull from the bog,

the marking of graves paved over,
when our seeded bodies
have fed the roots of trees,
or our ash beings seeding
a tear of rain.

How do we navigate eternity,
for our roots to tangle
and pull us into history,
aside from the knot of blood?
What art have I, apart from love.

A silent cabaret of faces
pass in a focus switch
through the viewing glass reflection.
Wire songbirds wait for me
in the next cabinet along.

A Boathouse

i.
        Itself, an oyster shell.
The wind calms into the lap of the bay,
        the wall rock desperate for the tide.
The swift daughters and sage rushes
        point & push with their colour,
the sky held out to its buoyant limit,
        so this point touches everything.

        A boathouse in Laugharne
is under this roof.
        There's a ghost in New York
smiling at this sky.
        All landscapes are familiar
                to the migrant bird.

ii.
        Sleep,
sleep within me, my x and y,
        I have no revelations for you now,
and the tides today have brought
        no new wrack to shore.
I don't have the faith to explain this,
        know you are loved.
If not always in memory,
        you will always be in beauty.

Reader & Listener

A breeze comes,
a delicate breath to
            cleaver the page.

I am reader
and listener.

Let the River Run Red

Let the river run red until the sea,
where the throat of a wild sky
washes to the reach
before the magnet dark of eve.

In this wavelength, this limbo hour,
the sea becomes its own country,
governed by the singing moon,
and the patience of the ribbon ground.

The alt-stars overlook
but don't quiver,
shaping out the living
from their knot across the bay.

I watch you Sun,

your dying sung by the burry gull
happy in its acid hymn,
empty as the love for a god
of too many things.

And as sand-step heals
crest to new moons, I trace my eyes
from the song dark and iron blue,
and offer the dying light
a sheltered place in my heart.

We Washed the Blood of Childhood From Our Faces

The stars over the house
had dug up their bones,
out from horizons
fallen away from their own spines
in the liberty of the morning last,
while loose throws from a pining god
skip & exit
the corner eye of the deepest August night.

We can still see the parchment sands
glow
and hear its hiss from our belly of wool,
wine, twice as deep as the night.

In the dark and drink,
in this open womb together,
stone tongues
begin to wet and flicker.
Our loving mouths speak.

We washed the blood of childhood
from our faces,
dried them, with our hands
at the fire pit
as would warming strangers.
In the tangling arms of woodsmoke,
our oil shale came alight
and sent the demons
to their ashes.

Our love was
in the turning of the earth.

What was lost, was not replaced
or forgotten
but we were
remembering ourselves.
Our scars already loved each other.

Love / West / Atlantic

We are as wide as sails,
bright, our silver bands to
the skipping rope line of the bay.

The Hush and crack,
hush and crack.

We walk
above the grit froth
of the backwash,
the black band
and cyan trace thread
of fishing line,
wind dried and tied
at the highest incline,
the furthest pull of the kneading moon.

In crack and hiss of the uprush
we could have walked
with one set of footsteps,
each ready to follow the other,
already stepping
into the other's stride,
looped by the umbilical love
of chapel hands, arms
folding around each other.

The sun break is still faint.
A star un-effecting.
No rays of worth
have yet reached out
to rub a little heat
into the lavender rocks,
stir the flower heads awake,
less the light of cornsilk
which carries these
delicate birds.

White feather

This sea
is older,
and the breeze,
older still.

Sands whisper,
'Goodnight',
now
your milk is light
to the darkness,

and each star speck
is a father's peck
on a daughter's head.

She is all the good in you,
with your cinnamon eyes
and my pear chin.

We see all the good
in the world
in our sharing dream,

and in all our celebrations
of wonder,

I'll be
the happy drunk.

Christopher Hopkins was born and grew up in Neath, South Wales. He has received an IPPY and two Pushcart Prize nomination for his debut chapbook *Take Your Journeys Home.* His second chapbook *The Last Time We Saw Strangers* was released in June 2018 and has been nominated for a Pushcart for its poem 'Iodine' and the chapbook itself nominated for the CLMP Firecracker Award. Christopher is widely published including poems in *The Morning Star, London Grip, Riggwelter Press, Ghost City Review, The Cortland Review, Indianapolis Review, Mojave River Review, Ink Sweat & Tears and Rust + Moth*. He currently lives in Kent, U.K.